Freedom

From

Porn Addiction

A Journey to Health and Healing

Susan J. McKinney

Susan J. McKinney

Copyright © 2023 by Susan J. McKinney

This book is intended for informational purposes only. The author and publisher shall have neither liability nor responsibility to any person or entity with respect to any loss or damage caused, or alleged to be caused, directly or indirectly by the information contained in this book. The information contained in this book is not intended as a substitute for professional medical advice, diagnosis, or treatment. Always seek the advice of your physician or other qualified health care provider with any questions you may have regarding a medical condition.

ISBN 9798374676709

Printed in the United States of America

Cover design by *Arlene van Roosmalen*

First edition, 2023

Dedication

This book is dedicated to all those who have been affected by porn addiction and are bravely on their journey to freedom, health, and healing. May this book serve as a source of hope, guidance and support on your path towards recovery.

And to those who love and support them, thank you for being there through the ups and downs. Together we can overcome this addiction and create a fulfilling, rewarding life in sobriety.

Foreword

"As a mental health professional, I have seen firsthand the devastating effects of porn addiction on individuals and their loved ones. It's a complex issue that is often misunderstood and stigmatized. This book, "Freedom from Porn Addiction: A Journey to Health and Healing," offers a comprehensive and compassionate look at the causes and effects of porn addiction, as well as practical strategies for overcoming it. It covers essential topics such as self-care, self-compassion, relapse prevention, and maintaining recovery." – **Susan J. McKinney**

"The author has done an excellent job of providing valuable information and guidance for those on the journey towards freedom from porn addiction. The book is written in an easy-to-understand and engaging style, making it accessible to a wide range of readers. The author also provides a holistic approach to the recovery process, addressing not only the addiction itself but also the underlying emotional and psychological issues that may have contributed to the development of the addiction." – **Robert L. Reyes**

"I highly recommend this book to anyone struggling with porn addiction, as well as to the loved ones of those who are affected by it. It's an invaluable resource that can provide hope, support and guidance on the journey towards health and healing." – **Kayla S. Brigman**

Table of Contents

Introduction

Welcome to "Freedom from Porn Addiction: A Journey to Health and Healing." If you're reading this book, you or someone you care about is likely struggling with an addiction to pornography. Porn addiction can be a difficult and isolating experience, but there is hope for recovery if you know you are not alone.

In this book, you'll find a comprehensive and compassionate guide to overcoming your addiction to pornography. I'll explore the root causes of porn addiction, how it can impact your life, and provide practical strategies and tools for breaking free and rebuilding your life.

Pornography addiction is a complex issue that affects people from all walks of life. Various factors, including stress, trauma, low self-esteem, and relationship problems, can trigger it. Aside from harming one's physical and mental health, it can also negatively affect one's relationships.

In this book, you'll discover how to handle those feelings to get back on track. I'll provide you with a thorough understanding of the nature of porn addiction and the latest research on how to overcome it effectively. You'll learn about the importance of self-care and how to build healthy coping mechanisms to deal with stress and other triggers.

I'll also explore the role of accountability and support in recovery and guide how to build a supportive network of friends, family members, and professionals who can help you on your journey. I'll cover the available treatment options, including therapy, support groups, and medication, and help you decide which approach is best for you.

Finally, I'll offer strategies for rebuilding your life and relationships after porn addiction. You'll learn how to repair the damage that your addiction may have caused and how to create a healthy and fulfilling life free from the constraints of pornography.

Whether you're just starting your journey to recovery or struggling with porn addiction for a while, this book is here to support and empower you. I'll offer guidance on how to seek help, cope with cravings and setbacks, and build a healthy and fulfilling life free from the constraints of porn addiction.

It's not easy to break free from an addiction, but it is possible with the proper support and determination. I believe in you, and I'm here to support you every step of the way. I'm excited to be a part of your journey to recovery and hope that this book will provide you with the tools and support you need to help you overcome your addiction and live a healthy and fulfilling life.

Let's start your journey to freedom and healing together!

Chapter I

Understanding Porn Addiction: Symptoms, Causes, and Consequences

"Porn addiction is not a real addiction; it's just a sign of weak willpower."

The statement above is a myth. Porn addiction is a real addiction and it's characterized by compulsive use of pornography despite negative consequences on personal, social and professional life. Research has shown that excessive use of pornography can lead to changes in brain function and structure similar to those seen in other addictions.

It's important to understand that addiction is a complex disease and can have multiple causes, including genetic, environmental, and psychological factors, and it's not just a matter of willpower.

Definition of Porn Addiction: Porn addiction is a compulsive and unhealthy use of pornography that interferes with an individual's daily life and relationships. It is characterized by a strong, uncontrollable urge to view pornography and difficulty reducing or stopping this behavior, even when it causes negative consequences.

Diagnostic and Statistical Manual of Mental Disorders (DSM-5) does not recognize porn addiction as a diagnosis, the standard reference manual used by mental health professionals to diagnose mental health conditions.

However, it is considered a behavioral addiction, similar to gambling or internet addiction. It can have severe consequences on an individual's psychological and physical health, as well as their relationships and overall well-being.

Porn addiction can take many different forms and can involve different types of pornography, including print, video, or online material. It can also apply different intensity and frequency levels, ranging from a mild problem to a severe and debilitating addiction.

It's important to note that viewing pornography itself is not necessarily unhealthy or problematic. However, when it becomes compulsive and interferes with an individual's daily life and relationships, it can be considered an addiction.

Porn addiction can be treated with various approaches, including therapy, support groups, medication, and self-help strategies. It is essential for individuals struggling with porn addiction to seek help from a qualified professional to overcome their addiction and rebuild their lives.

Symptoms of Porn Addiction

Porn addiction can manifest in a variety of different ways, and individuals may experience different combinations of symptoms. Some common symptoms of porn addiction include:

1. ***Compulsive use of pornography:***

An individual with porn addiction may feel an uncontrollable urge to view pornography and spend a significant amount of time doing so, even at the expense of other activities or responsibilities.

2. ***Difficulty controlling or reducing the use of pornography:***

An individual with porn addiction may have difficulty reducing or stopping their use of pornography, even when they want to. They may feel an intense craving for pornography and a lack of control over their behavior.

3. *Negative impacts on physical, mental, and emotional health:*

Porn addiction can significantly affect an individual's physical, mental, and emotional health. It can lead to problems such as sexual dysfunction, sleep problems, anxiety, depression, and shame.

4. *Negative impacts on relationships and social life:*

Porn addiction can also negatively impact an individual's relationships and social life. It can cause problems such as trust issues, communication problems, and social isolation.

Individuals with porn addiction may not necessarily exhibit all of these symptoms and may vary in intensity and frequency. It's also possible that an individual may not be aware of the extent or severity of their addiction.

Seeking help from a qualified professional can help an individual better understand their addiction and determine the best course of treatment.

Causes of Porn Addiction

Various factors can trigger porn addiction, and the specific causes can vary from person to person. Some common causes of porn addiction include:

1. ***Stress and anxiety:***

Stress and anxiety can be significant triggers for porn addiction. An individual may turn to pornography as a way to cope with stress or anxiety or use it to escape their problems.

2. ***Relationship issues:***

Relationship issues, such as conflict, mistrust, or lack of intimacy, can also trigger porn addiction. An individual may turn to pornography to cope with these issues or as a substitute for a real-life connection.

3. *Past trauma:*

Trauma, such as sexual abuse or other forms of abuse, can also be a factor in the development of porn addiction. A person may turn to pornography to cope with the pain or trauma of their past experiences.

4. *Low self-esteem or self-worth:*

Low self-esteem or self-worth can also be a factor in the development of porn addiction. An individual may turn to pornography as a way to cope with feelings of inadequacy or as a way to feel more powerful or in control.

5. *Easy access to pornography:*

The widespread availability of pornography online can also be a factor in the development of porn addiction. Individuals may be more likely to develop a habit if they have easy and constant access to pornography.

6. ***Genetics or brain chemistry:***

Research has also suggested that genes and brain chemistry contribute to porn addiction. Some individuals may be more prone to addiction due to their genetic makeup or how their brains process pleasure and reward.

It's important to note that porn addiction can be triggered by a combination of these and other factors, and the specific causes may vary from person to person. An effective treatment plan can be developed by understanding the root causes of addiction.

Consequences of Porn Addiction

Porn addiction can adversely affect a person's mental and physical health, as well as their relationships and overall well-being. Some expected outcomes of porn addiction include the following:

1. ***Negative impacts on mental health:***

Porn addiction can negatively impact an individual's mental health, including increased risk of depression, anxiety, and shame. These emotions may be fueled by feelings of guilt or self-loathing associated with the addiction and the negative consequences that it may have on relationships and other aspects of an individual's life.

2. ***Negative impacts on physical health:***

Porn addiction can also negatively impact an individual's physical health. It may contribute to problems such as sexual dysfunction, sleep problems, and other physical symptoms.

3. *Negative impacts on relationships:*

Porn addiction can negatively impact an individual's relationships, including trust issues, communication problems, and social isolation. It may also contribute to problems in romantic relationships, such as difficulties with intimacy or feelings of disconnection.

4. *Negative impacts on work or school performance:*

Porn addiction can also negatively impact an individual's performance at work or school. It may interfere with an individual's ability to concentrate, be productive, or meet their responsibilities.

It's important to note that the consequences of porn addiction can vary in severity and may not necessarily be present in every individual with this addiction. However, it is essential for individuals struggling with porn addiction to seek help to address these consequences and rebuild their lives.

The Importance of Seeking Help for Porn Addiction

Porn addiction is a complex and often isolating problem, and seeking help is paramount in overcoming it. Some reasons why seeking help for porn addiction is essential are as follows:

1. ***Porn addiction can have serious consequences:***

As previously mentioned, porn addiction can have severe consequences on an individual's mental and physical health, as well as their relationships and overall well-being. Seeking help can help individuals address these consequences and begin rebuilding their lives.

2. ***Porn addiction can be challenging to overcome on your own:***

Porn addiction is a complex problem that can be difficult to overcome on your own. It may require the guidance and support of a qualified professional to address the addiction's root causes and develop effective strategies for recovery.

3. ***Porn addiction is treatable:***

Porn addiction is treatable, and there are a variety of approaches that can be effective in helping an individual overcome their addiction. These approaches may include therapy, support groups, medication, or self-help strategies, and a qualified professional can help an individual determine the best procedure for their needs.

4. *Seeking help can provide hope:*

Porn addiction can be a demoralizing and isolating experience, and seeking help can give hope and support. It can be reassuring to know that others have struggled with similar problems and have been able to overcome their addiction with the help of qualified professionals.

In summary, seeking help for porn addiction is essential in overcoming this complex and often isolating problem. It can provide the support and guidance needed to address the root causes of the addiction and develop effective strategies for recovery. It can ultimately lead to a healthier and more fulfilling life.

Understanding the Causes and Effects of Porn Addiction on the Brain and Body

Porn addiction is a complex issue that affects individuals from all walks of life. It is a behavioral addiction characterized by the compulsive use of pornographic material, despite harmful consequences. In this section, we will explore the underlying causes and effects of porn addiction on the brain and body.

First, let's consider the causes of porn addiction. Research suggests that several factors contribute to the development of porn addiction, including:

- ***Genetics:***

Studies have found that individuals with a family history of addiction may be more susceptible to developing an addiction to porn.

- ***Brain chemistry:***

Research has shown that certain brain chemicals, such as dopamine, play a role in addiction. When an individual engages in compulsive porn use, the brain releases dopamine, creating a pleasurable sensation. Over time, the brain becomes accustomed to this flood of dopamine and requires more and more stimulation to achieve the same level of pleasure.

- ***Trauma:***

Individuals who have experienced traumatic events, such as sexual abuse, may be more likely to develop an addiction to porn as a coping mechanism.

- ***Mental health conditions:***

Individuals with mental health conditions, such as depression, anxiety, and ADHD, may be more susceptible to developing a porn addiction.

Effects of Porn Addiction on the Brain and Body

Now, let's look at the effects of porn addiction on the brain and body. These effects can be severe and long-lasting and can include the following:

- ***Changes in the brain:***

Research has shown that chronic porn use can change the brain's structure and function. These changes can affect how the brain processes pleasure, motivation, and decision-making.

- ***Erectile dysfunction:***

Excessive porn use can lead to erectile dysfunction and other sexual problems, such as premature ejaculation and difficulty achieving orgasm.

- ***Relationship problems:***

Porn addiction can hurt relationships, leading to feelings of isolation, mistrust, and resentment.

- ***Loss of productivity:***

Porn addiction can lead to a loss of productivity, as individuals may spend hours each day engaging in compulsive porn use.

- ***Mental health problems:***

Individuals with a porn addiction may experience various mental health problems, such as depression, anxiety, and shame.

Understanding the causes and consequences of porn addiction is essential to address and overcoming this addiction effectively.

In conclusion, porn addiction is a complex issue with many underlying causes and severe effects on the brain and body.

In the next chapter, we will discuss the impact of porn addiction on mental health.

Chapter 2

The Impact of Porn Addiction on Mental Health

Some of the ways porn addiction can affect your mental health are as follows:

- ***Increased risk of depression and anxiety:***

People addicted to porn are more likely to experience depression and anxiety. These mental health conditions may be fueled by feelings of shame, guilt, or self-loathing associated with the addiction and by the negative consequences that it may have on relationships and other aspects of an individual's life.

- ***Decreased self-esteem:***

Porn addiction can also lead to reduced self-esteem and a negative self-image. An individual may feel unworthy or inadequate due to addiction, contributing to a cycle of negative thinking and self-destructive behavior.

- ***Increased risk of other mental health problems:***

Porn addiction may also be associated with other mental health problems, such as obsessive-compulsive disorder (OCD), bipolar disorder, or post-traumatic stress disorder (PTSD).

- ***Negative impacts on cognition and brain functioning:***

Porn addiction has been linked to adverse effects on cognition and brain functioning, including impaired decision-making and problem-solving skills and decreased motivation and productivity.

The Importance of Addressing the Impact of Porn Addiction on Mental Health

Seeking treatment for mental health problems associated with porn addiction:

It is essential for individuals struggling with porn addiction to seek treatment for any mental health problems related to their addiction. In addition, they should also address these issues and improve their overall well-being.

Therapy's role in addressing the impact of porn addiction on mental health:

Therapy can be an effective tool in addressing the effects of porn addiction on mental health. It can provide an individual with a safe and supportive environment to explore their thoughts and feelings about their addiction. It can help them develop healthy coping mechanisms and strategies for managing their addiction.

The importance of self-care in addressing the impact of porn addiction on mental health:

Self-care is also essential in addressing the effects of porn addiction on mental health. This may involve exercise, healthy eating, sleep, and relaxation techniques, which can help individuals, manage stress and maintain their overall well-being.

The role of medication in addressing the impact of porn addiction on mental health:

In some cases, medication may be an appropriate treatment option for managing the effects of porn addiction on mental health. Antidepressants, for example, may help treat depression or anxiety associated with porn addiction.

It's important to note that medication should be used in conjunction with therapy and other treatment approaches and should be carefully monitored by a qualified healthcare professional.

The importance of addressing underlying issues that may contribute to porn addiction:

Porn addiction is often the result of underlying problems, such as stress, trauma, or low self-esteem, and addressing these issues is an essential aspect of overcoming the addiction.

Therapy can be an effective tool for exploring and addressing these underlying issues and helping individuals develop healthy coping mechanisms and strategies for managing their addiction.

The importance of self-forgiveness in overcoming porn addiction:

Porn addiction can be a demoralizing and isolating experience, and individuals may struggle with shame and guilt. It's essential for individuals to practice self-forgiveness and to recognize that addiction is a disease that requires treatment and support.

Seeking help and working on recovery can be an act of self-compassion and self-care and can ultimately lead to a healthier and more fulfilling life.

The Role of Shame and Guilt in the Addiction Cycle and How to Overcome Them

Shame and guilt are common emotions experienced by individuals struggling with porn addiction. These emotions can play a significant role in the addiction cycle and make it difficult for individuals to seek help and overcome their addiction.

In this section, we will explore the relationship between shame and guilt and porn addiction and discuss strategies for overcoming these emotions.

Shame

Shame is an emotion that is often described as a feeling of worthlessness or inadequacy. Individuals with a porn addiction may feel shame about their behavior and believe they are somehow "less than" or "not good enough" because of their addiction. This shame can lead to isolation and reluctance to seek help.

Guilt

On the other hand, guilt is an emotion related to a sense of responsibility or remorse for one's actions. Individuals with a porn addiction may feel guilty about their behavior's impact on themselves and those around them.

This guilt can lead to self-loathing and a belief that they are incapable of change.

It's essential to recognize that shame and guilt are not only normal emotions to have but can also be beneficial because they can motivate change, helping individuals take responsibility for their actions and seek help.

However, when these emotions are overwhelming, they can become a barrier to healing and recovery.

To overcome these emotions, you must understand that addiction is not a moral failing but a complex condition influenced by various factors, including genetics, brain chemistry, trauma, and mental health conditions.

Therefore, it's important to practice self-compassion and to remember that you are not alone and that help is available.

Another strategy for overcoming shame and guilt is to build a support system. This can include family and friends, support groups, and professional therapy.

In these settings, you can share your feelings and experiences without fear of judgment and learn from others who have been through similar experiences.

Additionally, learning about the science of addiction can also be helpful in understanding that addiction is a disease that affects your brain and it's not a moral failing.

Seeking professional help from a therapist or counselor specializing in addiction can also provide valuable support and guidance in overcoming these emotions.

However, by understanding the relationship between shame and guilt and addiction, and by building a support system, practicing self-compassion, and seeking professional help, individuals can overcome these emotions and begin the journey to health and healing.

In conclusion, shame and guilt are common emotions experienced by individuals with a porn addiction. These emotions can play a significant role in the addiction cycle and make it difficult to seek help and overcome the addiction.

Chapter 3

The Role of Emotional Intelligence in Overcoming Porn Addiction

The ability to recognize, understand and manage one's own and other's feelings constitutes emotional intelligence. It involves self-awareness, self-regulation, motivation, empathy, and social skills.

Here's how emotional intelligence can support recovery from porn addiction:

- ***Self-awareness:***

Developing self-awareness can help individuals better understand their own emotional experiences and triggers and can help them identify patterns of behavior that may contribute to their addiction.

- ***Self-regulation:***

Self-regulation can help individuals manage their emotions and behaviors and can help them develop healthy coping mechanisms to deal with stress and other triggers for their addiction.

- ***Motivation:***

Emotional intelligence can also help an individual develop inspiration and purpose, which can be crucial in recovery. It can help them set goals and work towards a healthy and fulfilling life, free from the constraints of their addiction.

- ***Empathy:***

Developing empathy can help an individual better understand and connect with others and can be crucial in repairing relationships that their addiction may have damaged.

- ***Social skills:***

Developing social skills can help an individual build a supportive network of friends, family members, and professionals who can help them on their journey to recovery.

The role of emotional intelligence in building healthy relationships:

Developing emotional intelligence can also be important in building healthy relationships, which can be a crucial component of recovery from porn addiction. It can help an individual develop trust, communication, and intimacy with others, which can be essential in repairing relationships that the habit may have damaged.

The role of emotional intelligence in setting boundaries:

Setting boundaries is an essential aspect of recovery from porn addiction, and emotional intelligence can be helpful in this process. It can help an individual recognize and respect their limits, as well as the limitations of others, and can help them communicate their boundaries effectively.

The role of emotional intelligence in self-care:

Emotional intelligence can also be important in self-care, which is an essential aspect of recovery from porn addiction. It can help an individual recognize and manage their own emotional needs. It can help them develop healthy coping mechanisms and strategies for managing stress and other triggers for their addiction.

The role of emotional intelligence in relapse prevention:

Relapse is a common challenge in recovery from porn addiction, and emotional intelligence can help prevent relapse. It can help individuals recognize and manage their emotions and behaviors and can help them develop healthy coping mechanisms to deal with stress and other triggers for their addiction.

Strategies for Developing Emotional Intelligence

Here are a few strategies for developing emotional intelligence to combat porn addiction:

1. **Practice mindfulness:**

Being mindful involves paying attention to the present moment and being aware of one's thoughts and emotions. It can be a helpful tool in developing emotional intelligence and can be practiced through activities such as meditation or yoga.

2. **Seek therapy:**

Therapy can be an effective tool for developing emotional intelligence. It can provide an individual with a safe and supportive environment to explore their thoughts and feelings and help them build self-awareness, self-regulation, and other emotional intelligence skills.

3. **Practice self-reflection:**

Self-reflection involves thinking about one's emotions and behaviors, which can be essential in developing emotional intelligence. It can help an individual better understand their own emotional experiences and triggers and can help them identify patterns of behavior that may contribute to their addiction.

4. *Seek feedback from others:*

Seeking input from others, such as friends, family members, or a therapist, can be a helpful tool in developing emotional intelligence. It can give an individual a different perspective on their emotions and behaviors and help them better understand how others perceive them.

5. *Engage in activities that foster emotional intelligence:*

Engaging in activities that foster emotional intelligence, such as reading, journaling, or participating in a support group, can also help develop these skills. These activities can provide an individual with a safe and supportive environment to explore their emotions and develop healthy coping mechanisms.

It's important to note that developing emotional intelligence is a process that takes time and practice. It may require patience and commitment, but it can ultimately lead to a healthier and more fulfilling life.

Developing Healthy Coping Mechanisms and Stress Management Techniques

One of the critical components of overcoming porn addiction is learning how to manage stress and develop healthy coping mechanisms. Stress can trigger compulsive porn use, and it can be difficult to maintain sobriety without practical coping strategies.

This section will explore the link between stress and porn addiction and discuss techniques for managing stress and developing healthy coping mechanisms.

Stress

Stress is a normal part of life, and it can come from various sources, such as work, relationships, financial difficulties, and personal problems. Research has shown that stress can be a significant trigger for compulsive porn use, as it can create feelings of anxiety, depression, and hopelessness.

Stress Management Techniques

To manage stress and reduce the risk of relapse, you must develop healthy coping mechanisms. These can include:

- ***Exercise:***

Regular exercise is an effective stress reliever and can help to improve mood and reduce anxiety.

- ***Relaxation techniques:***

Techniques such as deep breathing, meditation, and yoga can help to reduce stress and promote relaxation.

- ***Time management:***

Prioritizing tasks and managing time can help to reduce stress and improve productivity.

- ***Social support:***

Spending time with friends and family and participating in activities you enjoy can provide a sense of social support and help reduce stress.

- ***Professional Help:***

Seeking help from a therapist or counselor specializing in addiction can provide valuable support and guidance in managing stress.

It's also important to practice self-care, which means taking care of your physical, emotional, and mental well-being. Self-care can include getting enough sleep, eating a healthy diet, and engaging in activities you enjoy.

In addition, having a plan for dealing with triggers, such as identifying triggers, avoiding them or developing a plan to deal with them when they occur, can also be a very effective tool in managing stress and reducing the risk of relapse.

In conclusion, stress can be a significant trigger for compulsive porn use, and it's crucial to develop healthy coping mechanisms for managing stress. These can include exercise, relaxation techniques, time management, social support, self-care, and a plan to deal with triggers.

By learning how to manage stress, individuals with a porn addiction can reduce their risk of relapse and maintain their recovery.

Chapter 4

The Role of Support in Overcoming Porn Addiction

Porn addiction can be a complex and isolating problem, and seeking support can be essential to overcoming it. Support can give an individual hope and encouragement and help them feel less alone in their struggle.

Support can also provide an individual with practical assistance, such as help with childcare or transportation, which can help manage their addiction.

Types of support available to individuals recovering from porn addiction

- ***Therapy:***

Therapy can provide an individual with a safe and supportive environment to explore their thoughts and feelings about their addiction and help them develop healthy coping mechanisms and strategies for managing their addiction.

- ***Support groups:***

Support groups can give an individual a sense of community and support and help them feel less alone in their struggle. Support groups may be available through local organizations, online communities, or therapy programs.

- ***Family and friends:***

Family and friends can be a source of support and encouragement for an individual recovering from porn addiction. It's essential for individuals to communicate their needs and boundaries with their loved ones and to seek their support and understanding.

- *Professional support*:

Professional support, such as that provided by a therapist or addiction counselor, can also be an essential resource for individuals recovering from porn addiction. These professionals can provide guidance and support in managing addiction and rebuilding one's life.

Strategies for Building a Support Network

Below are crucial strategies for building a support network to help you in your fight against porn addiction.

1. *Identify supportive individuals:*

It's crucial for an individual recovering from porn addiction to identify supportive individuals who can provide encouragement and understanding. These may be family members, friends, or professionals.

2. *Communicate your needs:*

It's essential for an individual recovering from porn addiction to communicate their needs and boundaries with their support network. This can help ensure that they receive the support they need while respecting their limits.

3. *Seek out additional support resources:*

In addition to their support network, an individual recovering from porn addiction may also benefit from other support resources, such as therapy, support groups, or online communities.

These resources can provide additional guidance and support in managing the addiction and rebuilding one's life.

4. **Be open to trying new approaches:**

It's crucial for an individual recovering from porn addiction to try new approaches to building a support network. This may involve stepping outside one's comfort zone and trying new things, such as attending a support group or seeking therapy.

5. **Take care of yourself:**

Building a support network is essential to recovery from porn addiction, but it's also vital for an individual to prioritize self-care. This may involve exercise, healthy eating, sleep, and relaxation techniques, which can help manage stress and maintain your overall well-being.

In summary, building a support network will help you identify supportive individuals, communicate your needs, expose you to new approaches, and take care of your overall well-being.

Strategies for Setting Boundaries and Avoiding Triggers

An essential aspect of overcoming porn addiction is learning to set boundaries and avoid triggers. Triggers are specific cues or situations that can lead to a desire to engage in compulsive porn use. Setting boundaries and avoiding triggers can help reduce relapse risk and maintain recovery.

This section will explore the concept of triggers and discuss strategies for setting boundaries and avoiding them.

Triggers can be different for everyone, but some common examples include the following:

- ***Boredom:***

Feeling bored or unoccupied can lead to a desire to engage in compulsive porn use.

- ***Stress:***

Stress can be a significant trigger for compulsive porn use and can lead to a sense of hopelessness and anxiety.

- ***Loneliness:***

Feeling lonely or isolated can also be a trigger for compulsive porn use.

- ***Fatigue:***

Feeling tired or exhausted can also be a trigger for compulsive porn use.

Avoiding Triggers

To avoid triggers, you must learn how to set boundaries, which can include:

- ***Identifying triggers:***

Recognizing and understanding your triggers is the first step in avoiding them.

- ***Establishing boundaries:***

Establishing boundaries can include limiting when and where you will engage in compulsive porn use.

- ***Eliminating access:***

Removing or limiting access to pornographic material by using software or apps that block access to certain websites or by unfollowing social media accounts that post pornographic content.

- ***Building a support system:***

A support system can include reaching out to friends and family, participating in support groups, and seeking professional help.

- ***Finding healthy alternatives:***

Finding healthy options such as engaging in activities you enjoy, practicing self-care, and developing healthy coping mechanisms can help reduce the risk of relapse.

It's also essential to have a plan for when triggers occur. This plan can include having a list of healthy activities to engage in, having a list of people to call or talk to, or having a therapist or counselor on speed dial.

It's important to note that it's normal for triggers to happen, and it's a process; it's essential not to get discouraged and to keep working on developing those strategies.

In conclusion, triggers can be a significant barrier to overcoming porn addiction. By setting boundaries, avoiding triggers, and having a plan for when triggers occur, individuals with a porn addiction can reduce their risk of relapse and maintain their recovery.

Chapter 5

Understanding and Managing Cravings

Cravings are a normal part of recovery from any addiction, including porn addiction. Certain stimuli, such as stress, boredom, or feelings of loneliness, often trigger them. It's essential to recognize that cravings are a normal part of the recovery process and do not necessarily mean that an individual has failed or cannot overcome their addiction.

Several strategies can help manage cravings, and they are as follows:

- ***Identify triggers:***

One of the first steps in managing cravings is identifying the triggers that may be causing them. This may involve keeping a journal or using other methods to track one's thoughts, feelings, and behaviors. Once individuals have identified their triggers, they can develop strategies for managing them.

- ***Practice self-care:***

Self-care activities, such as exercise, healthy eating, sleep, and relaxation techniques, can help manage cravings. These activities enable individuals to manage stress and maintain their overall well-being.

- ***Seek support:***

Seeking support from a therapist, support group, or loved ones can also help manage cravings. These individuals can give an individual a sense of community and understanding and help them feel less alone in their struggle.

- ***Develop healthy coping mechanisms:***

It's essential for an individual recovering from porn addiction to develop healthy coping mechanisms for managing cravings. This may involve finding alternative activities to engage in when cravings occur, such as going for a walk or a hobby.

- ***Practice mindfulness techniques:***

Mindfulness techniques, such as deep breathing or visualization, can help manage cravings.

The role of medication in managing cravings:

In some cases, medication may be an appropriate treatment option. For example, certain medications may help reduce the intensity or frequency of cravings for specific substances, such as opioids or alcohol.

It's important to note that medication should be used in conjunction with therapy and other treatment approaches and should be carefully monitored by a qualified healthcare professional.

The need to develop a relapse prevention plan:

You can manage cravings and prevent relapse by developing a relapse prevention plan. A relapse prevention plan may include strategies such as identifying and managing triggers, seeking support when needed, and developing healthy coping mechanisms.

It's crucial for an individual recovering from porn addiction to have a clear plan to manage cravings and prevent relapse.

The role of motivation in managing cravings:

Motivation is an essential factor in managing cravings and overcoming porn addiction. It can help an individual stay committed to recovery and work towards a healthy and fulfilling life. Strategies for maintaining motivation may include:

- Setting goals.
- Finding meaning and purpose in one's recovery journey.
- Seeking inspiration and encouragement from others.

The importance of patience and persistence in managing cravings:

Managing cravings and overcoming porn addiction can be challenging, and an individual needs to be patient and persistent in their efforts. It may take time to develop effective strategies for managing cravings, and individuals need to be kind to themselves and recognize that recovery is a journey.

Building a Support System and Seeking Professional Help

Overcoming a porn addiction can be a challenging and complex process. A support system can provide valuable encouragement and guidance and help individuals maintain their recovery.

In this section, we will explore the importance of building a support system and seeking professional help in overcoming porn addiction.

A support system can include various people, such as family members, friends, and support groups. These individuals can provide a listening ear, offer words of encouragement, and provide a sense of community and understanding.

Support groups can be beneficial, as they provide a safe space for individuals to share their experiences, feelings, and challenges without fear of judgment.

Another critical aspect of building a support system is seeking professional help. A therapist or counselor specializing in addiction can provide valuable support and guidance in overcoming porn addiction.

They can help individuals understand the underlying causes of their addiction, develop healthy coping mechanisms, and create a personalized treatment plan.

In addition, medication can also be a valuable tool in the recovery process. Medication-assisted treatment (MAT) is a treatment option that combines medications with therapy to treat addiction. This treatment can help individuals to manage withdrawal symptoms, reduce cravings, and improve overall recovery outcomes.

It's important to note that professional help can come in different forms, and it's crucial to find the right fit for you. This can include individual therapy, group therapy, or online therapy. It can also have different modalities, such as cognitive behavioral therapy, mindfulness-based therapy, and motivational interviewing.

Support from family and friends, support groups, and professional therapy can provide valuable encouragement and guidance and help individuals maintain their recovery.

It's essential to find the right fit for you and to stay encouraged if the first attempt doesn't work; it may take some trial and error to find the right fit.

In conclusion, building a support system and seeking professional help is essential to overcoming porn addiction.

Chapter 6

The Importance of Self-Care in Recovery

Self-care is taking care of one's physical, mental, and emotional well-being. It involves engaging in activities that promote overall health and well-being, including exercise, healthy eating, sleep, and relaxation techniques.

Self-care is an essential aspect of recovery from porn addiction. It can help an individual manage stress and other challenges that may arise in the recovery process and can also help them maintain their overall well-being.

Strategies for Practicing Self-Care

There are many strategies that an individual can use to practice self-care in recovery from porn addiction. Some examples include:

- ***Exercise:***

Exercise can be an effective tool for managing stress and promoting overall well-being. It can help an individual feel more energized and motivated and improve their physical health.

- ***Healthy eating:***

Eating a healthy diet is an essential aspect of self-care. It can help individuals feel more energized and focused and improve their physical health.

- ***Sleep:***

Adequate sleep is essential for overall well-being and can be especially important in the recovery from porn addiction. An individual must prioritize getting enough sleep and develop healthy sleep habits.

- ***Relaxation techniques:***

Breathing deeply, practicing meditation, or taking part in yoga can help manage stress and promote well-being.

The role of self-care in managing triggers:

Self-care can be an essential tool in managing triggers for porn addiction. Taking care of one's physical, mental, and emotional well-being can better handle stress and other challenges that may arise in recovery.

The importance of finding balance in self-care:

It's essential for an individual recovering from porn addiction to find a balance in their self-care practices. This may involve finding a balance between activities that promote relaxation and those that encourage productivity or between enjoyable and more challenging exercises.

The role of self-care in building a healthy and fulfilling life:

Self-care is essential to building a healthy and fulfilling life after overcoming porn addiction. By taking care of one's well-being, one can work towards a fulfilling and meaningful life and better achieve their goals and aspirations.

The importance of self-compassion in self-care:

Self-compassion is an essential aspect of self-care. It involves being kind and understanding towards oneself and recognizing that everyone has flaws and weaknesses. Individuals who practice self-compassion are more resilient and better able to cope with challenges that may arise during their recovery process.

Rebuilding and Moving Forward

Overcoming porn addiction involves more than just stopping the behavior; it also consists in rebuilding one's life in a healthy and fulfilling manner. Several strategies can help rebuild one's life after overcoming porn addiction:

- ***Set goals:***

Setting goals can be essential in rebuilding one's life. These goals may be related to one's career, relationships, health, or other areas of life. Setting goals can help an individual focus on the future and work towards a healthy and fulfilling life.

- ***Seek therapy:***

Therapy can be an essential resource in rebuilding one's life after overcoming porn addiction. It can provide an individual with a safe and supportive environment to explore their thoughts and feelings and help them develop healthy coping mechanisms and strategies for managing stress and other challenges.

- ***Build a support network:***

Building a supportive network of friends, family members, and professionals can be essential to rebuilding one's life. This network can provide an individual with encouragement, guidance, and practical assistance as they work towards their goals.

- ***Practice self-care:***

Practicing self-care is critical to rebuilding one's life after overcoming porn addiction. This may involve exercise, healthy eating, sleep, and relaxation techniques.

- ***Seek out new opportunities:***

Seeking out new opportunities, such as education or career development, can be essential in rebuilding one's life after overcoming porn addiction. These opportunities give individuals a sense of purpose and direction and help them work towards a healthy and fulfilling future.

The Impact of Porn Addiction on Relationships and Intimacy

Porn addiction can have a significant impact on relationships and intimacy. The compulsive use of pornographic material can lead to feelings of isolation, mistrust, and resentment and ultimately damage or destroy relationships.

In this section, we will explore the impact of porn addiction on relationships and intimacy and discuss strategies for overcoming these challenges.

Porn addiction can hurt relationships in several ways, such as:

- ***Lack of intimacy:***

Compulsive porn use can lead to a lack of interest in real-life sexual experiences and ultimately damage or destroy relationships.

- ***Trust issues:***

Porn addiction can lead to mistrust and betrayal in relationships, as individuals may keep their addiction a secret.

- ***Communication breakdown:***

Difficulty in communicating about the addiction, feelings and needs can lead to a breakdown in communication within the relationship.

- ***Isolation:***

Individuals with a porn addiction may withdraw from social activities and become isolated from friends and family.

To overcome these challenges, you must be open and honest with your partner about your addiction and its impact on your relationship. This can be a complex and emotional process, but it's essential to rebuilding trust and intimacy.

Another important aspect is improving communication and intimacy within the relationship. This can include setting aside time to talk and connect, engaging in activities together, and working on rebuilding trust and intimacy.

Seeking professional help can also be a vital step in overcoming the impact of porn addiction on relationships and intimacy. A therapist or counselor who specializes in addiction and relationships can provide valuable support and guidance in rebuilding trust and intimacy and can help couples navigate the challenges that come with addiction.

It's also important to remember that healing and rebuilding relationships takes time, patience and work from both parties. It's important to be kind and compassionate with yourself and your partner and to understand that recovery is a process that requires time, effort and patience.

In conclusion, porn addiction can significantly impact relationships and intimacy. By being open and honest with their partner, working on improving communication and intimacy, seeking professional help, and being patient and compassionate with yourself and your partner, individuals can overcome these challenges and rebuild trust and intimacy in their relationships.

Chapter 7

Creating a Porn-Free Environment: Strategies for Staying on Track

The importance of creating a porn-free environment is vital in your fight against overcoming porn addiction. To effectively overcome porn addiction, an individual must create a porn-free climate.

This may involve taking steps such as removing any pornography from their home, blocking access to porn websites, and avoiding triggers that may lead to viewing pornography.

Several strategies can help stay on track in recovery from porn addiction:

1. **Develop a relapse prevention plan:**

Individuals can use it to manage their recovery and prevent relapses. It may include techniques such as identifying and managing triggers, seeking support when needed, and developing healthy coping mechanisms.

2. **Seek support:**

Seeking support from a therapist, support group, or loved ones can be vital to staying on track in recovery. These individuals can provide an individual with encouragement, guidance, and a sense of community as they work towards their goals.

3. **Practice self-care:**

Practicing self-care is essential to staying on track in recovery. This may involve exercise, healthy eating, sleep, and relaxation techniques, which can help an addict, manage stress and maintain their overall well-being.

4. *Find meaning and purpose:*

Finding meaning and purpose in one's recovery journey can be an essential aspect of staying on track. This may involve setting goals, finding fulfilling and meaningful activities, or seeking inspiration and guidance from others.

5. *The importance of patience and persistence:*

Staying on track in recovery from porn addiction can be challenging, and an individual needs to be patient and persistent in their efforts. It may take time to develop effective strategies for managing recovery, and an individual needs to be kind to themselves and recognize that recovery is a journey.

The role of accountability in staying on track:

Accountability can be an essential tool in recovering from porn addiction. Keeping accountability to one's recovery goals may involve seeking support from a therapist, support group, or accountability partner.

The importance of building healthy habits:

Building healthy habits can be an essential aspect of staying on track in recovery. This may involve developing routines and practices that promote well-being, such as exercise, healthy eating, and sufficient sleep.

The role of motivation in staying on track:

Motivation is essential in staying on track in recovery from porn addiction. It can help an individual stay committed to healing and working towards a healthy and fulfilling life.

Strategies for maintaining motivation may include:

- Setting goals.
- Finding meaning and purpose in one's recovery journey.
- Seeking inspiration and encouragement from others.

The importance of forgiveness in staying on track:

Forgiveness can be essential to staying on track in recovery from porn addiction. This may involve forgiving oneself for any mistakes or setbacks that may occur in the recovery process and forgiving others who may have contributed to the addiction.

By practicing forgiveness, individuals can let go of negative emotions and focus on moving forward in their recovery journey.

The Role of Therapy in Recovery

Therapy is a treatment process involving working with a trained mental health professional to address mental health issues and challenges. The importance of therapy in recovery from porn addiction cannot be overstated. Therapy can be an essential resource in recovery from porn addiction.

It can provide an individual with a safe and supportive environment to explore their thoughts and feelings and help them develop healthy coping mechanisms and strategies for managing stress and other challenges.

Many different types of therapy can be helpful in recovery from porn addiction. Some examples include:

1. *Cognitive-behavioral therapy (CBT):*

CBT aims to change negative thinking patterns and behaviors. It can be especially helpful in recovery from porn addiction, as it can help an individual identify and change behaviors that contribute to their addiction.

2. *Dialectical behavior therapy (DBT):*

DBT is a type of therapy that combines CBT with mindfulness and acceptance-based strategies. It can be helpful in recovery from porn addiction, as it can help an individual learn to manage their emotions and behaviors healthily.

3. *Psychoanalytic therapy:*

This therapy focuses on exploring an individual's unconscious thoughts and feelings. Recovery from porn addiction can be made more accessible by understanding the underlying causes of the habit.

4. *Family therapy:*

Family therapy can be an essential resource in recovering from porn addiction, as it can help individuals repair and strengthen their relationships with family members.

It is crucial for an individual recovering from porn addiction to find the right therapy for their needs. This may involve trying different therapies or working with other therapists until an individual finds a treatment approach that works for them.

Overcoming Co-occurring Mental Health Conditions Such as Depression and Anxiety

Porn addiction is often accompanied by co-occurring mental health conditions such as depression and anxiety. These conditions can make it more challenging to overcome an addiction and can also worsen the symptoms of the addiction.

This section will explore the link between porn addiction and co-occurring mental health conditions and discuss strategies for overcoming these conditions.

Depression and anxiety are common mental health conditions that can occur alongside a porn addiction. They can be caused by a variety of factors, such as:

- ***Brain chemistry:***

Research has shown that certain brain chemicals, such as dopamine, play a role in addiction and mental health conditions.

- ***Trauma:***

Trauma can lead to both addiction and mental health conditions.

- ***Genetics:***

Individuals with a family history of addiction or mental health conditions may be more susceptible to developing a porn addiction and co-occurring mental health conditions.

To overcome co-occurring mental health conditions, you must seek professional help. A therapist or counselor who specializes in addiction and mental health can provide valuable support and guidance in understanding and treating these conditions.

Medication-assisted treatment (MAT) can also be valuable in treating co-occurring mental health conditions. Medications such as antidepressants, antipsychotics, and anti-anxiety medications can help to manage symptoms and improve overall recovery outcomes.

It's also essential to address the underlying causes of mental health conditions and addiction, such as trauma. This can include therapy modalities such as cognitive behavioral therapy, talk therapy, and dialectical behavioral therapy.

In addition, self-care practices can also help manage symptoms of depression and anxiety. These include exercise, relaxation techniques, and mindfulness practices such as meditation and yoga.

It's important to remember that treating co-occurring conditions is a process, and it's essential not to get discouraged if the first attempt doesn't work; it may take some trial and error to find the right fit.

In conclusion, overcoming co-occurring mental health conditions such as depression and anxiety is essential to overcoming porn addiction. By seeking professional help, utilizing medication-assisted treatment, addressing underlying causes, and practicing self-care, individuals can improve their recovery outcomes and manage the symptoms of these conditions.

Chapter 8

Healing from the Damage of Porn Addiction: Repairing Relationships and Rebuilding Trust

Porn addiction can significantly impact an individual's relationships, including damaging trust, communication, and intimacy. As well as feeling ashamed, guilty, and disconnected, it can also cause feelings of shame, guilt, and isolation.

Healing from the damage of porn addiction is an essential aspect of recovery. It involves repairing relationships and rebuilding trust and can help an individual feel more connected and fulfilled in their relationships.

Several strategies can be helpful in healing from the damage of porn addiction and rebuilding trust in relationships:

- ***Seek therapy:***

Therapy can be an essential resource in healing from the damage of porn addiction and rebuilding trust. It can provide an individual with tools and strategies for improving communication, trust, and intimacy in their relationships.

- ***Practice honesty and transparency:***

Honesty and openness are essential in rebuilding trust in relationships. It's crucial for an individual to be open and honest about their recovery journey and to communicate their needs and boundaries with their loved ones.

- ***Seek support:***

Seeking support from a support group or loved ones can be essential to healing and rebuilding trust in relationships. These individuals can provide an individual with encouragement, guidance, and a sense of community as they work towards their goals.

- ***Practice forgiveness:***

Forgiveness can be an essential tool in healing from the damage of porn addiction and rebuilding trust in relationships. This may involve forgiving oneself for any mistakes or setbacks that may occur in the recovery process and forgiving others who may have contributed to the addiction.

- ***Build trust:***

Trust is an essential aspect of healthy relationships. It's vital for an individual to be reliable, dependable, and trustworthy in their relationships and to work towards rebuilding trust if it has been damaged.

- ***The importance of patience and persistence:***

Healing from the damage of porn addiction and rebuilding trust in relationships can be challenging, and an individual needs to be patient and persistent in their efforts.

The role of communication in healing and rebuilding trust:

Communication is essential to healing from the damage of porn addiction and rebuilding trust in relationships. It's necessary for an individual to be open and honest about their recovery journey and to be willing to listen to the thoughts and feelings of their loved ones.

It's also important to practice effective communication skills, such as being clear and specific in expressing one's needs and boundaries and being open to hearing the perspectives of others.

The importance of boundaries in healing and rebuilding trust:

Boundaries are essential in healing from the damage of porn addiction and rebuilding trust in relationships. It's crucial for an individual to establish healthy boundaries with their loved ones and to communicate their needs and boundaries.

This may involve setting limits on specific behaviors or activities or setting aside time for self-care and personal growth.

The role of forgiveness in healing and rebuilding trust:

Forgiveness is essential to healing from the damage of porn addiction and rebuilding trust in relationships. Individuals can benefit from forgiving themselves for past mistakes and setbacks and forgiving others who may have contributed to their addiction.

By practicing forgiveness, individuals can let go of negative emotions and focus on rebuilding trust in their relationships.

The importance of self-care in healing and rebuilding trust:

Self-care is essential to healing from the damage of porn addiction and rebuilding trust in relationships. It's vital for an individual to prioritize their well-being and to engage in activities that promote overall health and well-being.

This can help an individual feel more resilient and better equipped to cope with the challenges that may arise in recovery.

Building and Maintaining Healthy Relationships

Building and maintaining healthy relationships is essential to recovery from porn addiction. Healthy relationships can provide an individual with support, guidance, and a sense of belonging and help them feel more connected and fulfilled.

Several strategies can help build and maintain healthy relationships in recovery from porn addiction:

1. **Seek therapy:**

Therapy can be essential in building and maintaining healthy relationships. It can provide an individual with tools and strategies for improving communication, trust, and intimacy in their relationships.

2. Practice transparency and honesty:

Honesty and transparency are fundamental in building and maintaining healthy relationships. It's essential for an individual to be open and honest about their recovery journey and to communicate their needs and boundaries with their loved ones.

3. Seek moral support:

Seeking support from a support group or loved ones can be critical to building and maintaining healthy relationships. These individuals can provide an individual with encouragement, guidance, and a sense of community as they work towards their goals.

4. Practice forgiveness:

Forgiveness can be essential in building and maintaining healthy relationships. This may involve forgiving oneself for any mistakes or setbacks that may occur in the recovery process and forgiving others who may have contributed to the addiction.

5. *Build trust:*

Trust is a paramount aspect of healthy relationships. It's crucial for an individual to be reliable, dependable, and trustworthy in their relationships and to work towards rebuilding trust if it has been damaged.

It's vital for an individual recovering from porn addiction to find balance in their relationships. This may involve finding a balance between time spent with loved ones and time spent on self-care or between enjoyable and more challenging activities.

Understanding the Role of Trauma in the Development of a Porn Addiction

Trauma can play a significant role in the development of porn addiction. Trauma can include experiences such as sexual abuse, physical abuse, emotional abuse, or neglect.

These experiences can lead to feelings of shame, guilt, and a sense of hopelessness, which can ultimately contribute to the development of an addiction.

This section will explore the link between trauma and porn addiction and discuss strategies for addressing and overcoming this connection.

Trauma can lead to several emotional and psychological issues contributing to the development of porn addiction. These can include:

- ***Low self-esteem and self-worth:***

Trauma can lead to feelings of worthlessness and inadequacy, which can be a significant factor in the development of an addiction.

- ***Difficulty in managing emotions:***

Trauma can affect the ability to manage emotions healthily, leading to addiction as a coping mechanism.

- ***Difficulty in trusting others:***

Trauma can lead to difficulty in trusting others, which can contribute to feelings of isolation and a lack of social support.

To address and overcome the connection between trauma and porn addiction, you must seek professional help. A therapist or counselor who specializes in trauma and addiction can provide valuable support and guidance in understanding and treating the connection between the two.

Trauma-focused therapies such as cognitive behavioral therapy, eye movement desensitization and reprocessing (EMDR) and dialectical behavioral therapy (DBT) can help address the underlying causes of addiction, such as trauma.

It's also important to practice self-care and self-compassion. This can include engaging in activities you enjoy, spending time with loved ones, and setting boundaries to protect yourself from further trauma.

In addition, it's important to remember that healing from trauma is a process, and it may take time and patience; it's essential not to get discouraged and to keep seeking help, support and guidance.

In conclusion, understanding the role of trauma in the development of porn addiction is an essential aspect of overcoming an addiction.

By seeking professional help, utilizing trauma-focused therapies, practicing self-care, and being patient and compassionate with yourself, individuals can begin to address the underlying causes of their addiction and move towards healing and recovery.

The Importance of Self-Care and Self-Compassion in Recovery

Self-care and self-compassion are critical components of recovery from addiction. Self-care refers to the actions and practices individuals engage in to maintain and improve their physical, emotional, and mental well-being.

Self-compassion, on the other hand, refers to treating oneself with kindness, understanding, and empathy. Together, self-care and self-compassion can provide a strong foundation for recovery and aid in healing.

Self-care is essential for recovery, as addiction can affect the individual's physical and emotional well-being. Self-care practices such as exercise, getting enough sleep, eating a healthy diet, and engaging in activities that one enjoys can help to improve overall well-being, reduce stress, and improve mood.

Additionally, self-care practices can help counteract the adverse effects of addiction on the body and mind, such as anxiety and depression.

Self-compassion is also crucial for recovery, as addiction can lead to feelings of shame and self-loathing. Self-compassion allows individuals to treat themselves with kindness and understanding, which can help counteract addiction's adverse effects on self-esteem. Self-compassion can also help individuals accept their past mistakes, forgive themselves and move forward positively.

Self-compassion can also be a powerful tool in reducing the risk of relapse, as it can help individuals to be more resilient in the face of triggers and setbacks.

When individuals can be kind and understanding towards themselves, they are less likely to engage in self-destructive behaviors and more likely to seek out healthy coping mechanisms.

In addition, self-care and self-compassion can also aid in healing any underlying emotional and psychological issues that may have contributed to the development of addiction, such as trauma and low self-esteem.

By treating oneself with kindness and understanding, individuals can address these underlying issues and move towards healing and recovery.

It's important to note that self-care and self-compassion are ongoing practices, not just one-time activities. Incorporating self-care and self-compassion into daily life is crucial for maintaining recovery and well-being.

This can include setting aside time each day for self-care activities, practicing mindfulness and self-compassionate thoughts, and seeking out professional help if needed.

Incorporating self-care and self-compassion into daily life is crucial for maintaining recovery and well-being and should be considered an ongoing practice rather than a one-time activity.

In conclusion, self-care and self-compassion are essential components of recovery from addiction. They provide a strong foundation for recovery, aid in the healing process, and can reduce the risk of relapse.

Chapter 9

Finding the Right Treatment Approach for You

Finding the right treatment approach for overcoming porn addiction is essential to recovery. The proper strategy will vary from person to person and may involve a combination of different treatment modalities.

There are several types of treatment approaches that can help overcome porn addiction. Some examples include:

- ***Cognitive-behavioral therapy (CBT):***

CBT helps people identify and change their negative behaviors and thinking patterns. It can be especially helpful in recovery from porn addiction, as it can help an individual identify and change behaviors that contribute to their addiction.

- ***Dialectical behavior therapy (DBT):***

DBT is a type of therapy that combines CBT with mindfulness and acceptance-based strategies. It can be helpful in recovery from porn addiction, as it can help an individual learn to manage their emotions and behaviors healthily.

- ***Psychoanalytic therapy:***

This therapy focuses on exploring an individual's unconscious thoughts and feelings. An individual can gain insight into the underlying causes of their addiction by using it in recovery from porn addiction.

- ***Family therapy:***

Family therapy can be an essential resource in recovery from porn addiction, as it can help individuals repair and strengthen their relationships with family members.

Factors to Consider When Choosing a Treatment Approach

There are several factors that an individual should consider when choosing a treatment approach for overcoming porn addiction. These may include:

- ***Personal preferences:***

An individual needs to choose a treatment approach that aligns with their personal preferences and values. This may involve considering things such as the type of therapy that feels most comfortable, the therapist's style, and the treatment's location.

- ***The severity of the addiction:***

The severity of an individual's porn addiction can be an essential factor to consider when choosing a treatment approach. For example, someone with a more severe addiction may require more intensive treatment, such as inpatient care or a longer course of therapy.

- ***Other mental health concerns:***

If an individual has other mental health concerns besides their porn addiction, it's fundamental to consider these when choosing a treatment approach. A treatment approach that addresses multiple concerns may be more effective.

Support groups can be an essential resource in recovery from porn addiction. They can provide an individual with a sense of community and support as they work towards their recovery goals.

Several types of support groups are available, including 12-step groups, such as Sex Addicts Anonymous, and non-12-step groups, such as Sex and Love Addicts Anonymous. Individuals must choose a support group that aligns with their personal preferences and needs.

Overcoming porn addiction is often a long-term process, and individuals must consider ongoing treatment in their recovery journey. This may involve continuing with therapy, attending support groups, or engaging in other forms of ongoing support, such as working with a coach or mentor.

In some cases, medication may be an essential aspect of treatment for porn addiction. For example, certain medications, such as selective serotonin reuptake inhibitors (SSRIs), may help manage underlying mental health concerns, such as depression or anxiety, that may contribute to an individual's addiction.

It's crucial for an individual to discuss the potential use of medication with a mental health professional and to consider the potential risks and benefits carefully.

Finding a treatment team that is supportive and collaborative can be an essential aspect of recovery from porn addiction. This may involve working with a therapist and possibly other professionals, like a physician or nutritionist or attending a support group to help create a comprehensive treatment plan.

Individuals need to find a treatment team that they feel comfortable with, and that is committed to their recovery.

• **Navigating Life After Porn Addiction**

Life after overcoming porn addiction can present its own set of challenges. Individuals may face temptations and triggers and need to navigate relationships and other aspects of their life differently.

Several strategies can help navigate life after overcoming porn addiction:

1. ***Seek support:***

Seeking support from a therapist, support group, or loved ones can be essential to navigating life after porn addiction. These individuals can provide an individual with encouragement, guidance, and a sense of community as they work towards their goals.

2. *Practice self-care:*

Practicing self-care is essential to navigating life after porn addiction. This may involve exercise, healthy eating, sleep, and relaxation techniques, which can help manage stress and maintain overall well-being.

3. *Build healthy habits:*

Building healthy habits can be crucial to navigating life after porn addiction. This may involve developing routines and practices that promote well-being, such as exercise, healthy eating, and sufficient sleep.

4. *Find meaning and purpose:*

Finding meaning and purpose in one's recovery journey can be an essential aspect of navigating life after porn addiction. This may involve setting goals, finding fulfilling activities or seeking inspiration and guidance from others.

5. *Practice gratitude:*

Practicing gratitude can be essential to navigating life after porn addiction. It involves focusing on the positive aspects of one's life and being thankful for what one has. This can help individuals feel more positive and hopeful as they navigate life after overcoming addiction.

Navigating life after overcoming porn addiction can be challenging, and an individual needs to be patient and persistent in their efforts. It may take time to develop effective strategies for managing recovery, and an individual needs to be kind to themselves and recognize that recovery is a journey.

Relapse Prevention and Maintaining Recovery

Relapse is a common occurrence in the recovery process from addiction. It's important to understand that relapse is not a failure but a part of the recovery process.

In this section, we will explore the topic of relapse prevention and maintaining recovery from addiction.

Relapse prevention is identifying triggers and developing strategies to cope with them. Triggers can be different for everyone, but some common examples include the following:

- ***Stress*:**

Stress can be a significant trigger for addiction and can lead to a sense of hopelessness and anxiety.

- ***Boredom*:**

Feeling bored or unoccupied can lead to a desire to engage in compulsive use of addictive substances or behavior.

- ***Loneliness*:**

Feeling lonely or isolated can also be a trigger for addiction.

- ***Fatigue*:**

Feeling tired or exhausted can also be a trigger for addiction.

Preventing Relapse

To prevent relapse, you must develop a plan of action that includes the following:

- ***Identifying triggers:***

Recognizing and understanding your triggers is the first step in avoiding them.

- ***Establishing boundaries:***

Establishing boundaries can include setting limits on when and where you will engage in compulsive use of addictive substances or behavior.

- ***Building a support system:***

A support system can include reaching out to friends and family, participating in support groups, and seeking professional help.

- ***Finding healthy alternatives:***

Finding healthy options such as engaging in activities you enjoy, practicing self-care, and developing healthy coping mechanisms can help reduce the risk of relapse.

It's also essential to have a plan for when triggers occur. This can include having a list of healthy activities to engage in, having a list of people to call or talk to, or having a therapist or counselor on speed dial.

Maintaining Recovery

In addition to relapse prevention, it's also essential to maintain recovery by:

- Continuously working on oneself and one's recovery journey can include therapy, support groups, and self-help techniques.

- Building a solid support system and having a positive social network

- Practicing self-care and self-compassion.

- Setting goals and working towards them.

- Continuously educating oneself about addiction, recovery and ways to maintain recovery.

Maintaining recovery also includes ongoing self-improvement, building a solid support system, practicing self-care and self-compassion, setting goals and continually educating oneself about addiction and recovery.

It's important to remember that recovery is a lifelong process and requires ongoing effort and commitment.

In conclusion, relapse is a common occurrence in the recovery process from addiction. By understanding the triggers and developing strategies to cope with them, individuals can reduce the risk of relapse and maintain their recovery.

How to Find and Maintain Motivation for Change

Motivation is a critical component in the process of change. Motivation can make it easier to take the necessary steps towards achieving goals and making positive changes in one's life.

Finding and maintaining motivation for change can be challenging, but several strategies can help.

One way to find motivation for change is to set clear, specific, and achievable goals. This can give direction and purpose to the change process. It's essential to ensure the goals are realistic, measurable, and have a time frame.

A clear idea of what you want to achieve can increase motivation and drive towards change.

Another way to find motivation for change is to focus on the benefits of change. This can include the positive impact on one's health, relationships, and overall well-being.

Reflecting on the potential benefits of change can increase motivation and drive towards achieving goals.

It's also essential to develop a plan of action to achieve goals. This can include breaking down goals into smaller, manageable tasks, setting deadlines, and creating a schedule to work on assignments.

Having a plan in place can help to increase motivation and drive towards change by providing a sense of direction and purpose.

Another strategy for finding motivation for change is to build a support system. This can include seeking out the support of friends, family, and professionals.

A supportive network can provide encouragement, guidance, and accountability, which can be essential for maintaining motivation and driving towards change.

It's important to note that motivation is not a constant state and can fluctuate. Maintaining motivation can be challenging, but several strategies can help. Some strategies include:

- Reminding oneself of the reasons why change is essential and the benefits that come with it.

- Celebrating small successes along the way

- Being kind and compassionate with oneself, avoiding self-criticism and self-doubt

- Reflecting on progress and progress made

- Finding inspiration in others who have achieved similar goals

Setting clear, specific, and achievable goals, focusing on the benefits of change, developing a plan of action, building a support system, and reminding oneself of the reasons why change is important, and the benefits that come with it can help to increase motivation and drive towards change.

It's important to remember that motivation is not a constant state, and it can fluctuate, so it's important to be patient and compassionate with oneself, keep going and seek help if needed.

In conclusion, motivation is a critical component in the process of change. Finding and maintaining motivation can be challenging, but several strategies can help.

Chapter 10

Maintaining Sobriety and Living a Fulfilling Life in Recovery

Maintaining sobriety is an essential aspect of recovery from porn addiction. It involves abstaining from the behaviors and activities contributing to the addiction and working towards a healthy and fulfilling life.

Several strategies can help maintain sobriety from porn addiction:

1. *Attend support groups:*

Attendance at support groups, such as 12-step or non-12-step groups, can be essential to maintaining sobriety from porn addiction. These groups provide individuals with community, support and accountability as they work towards their recovery goals.

2. *Practice self-care:*

Practicing self-care is essential to maintaining sobriety from porn addiction. This may involve exercise, healthy eating, sleep, and relaxation techniques, which can help support their overall well-being.

3. *Build healthy habits:*

Building healthy habits can be essential to maintaining sobriety from porn addiction. This may involve developing routines and practices that promote well-being, such as exercise, healthy eating, and sufficient sleep.

4. *Seek professional help:*

Seeking professional help, such as therapy or coaching, can also help maintain sobriety from porn addiction. These professionals can provide an individual with tools and strategies for managing recovery and building a healthy and fulfilling life.

5. ***Develop a support network:***

Developing a support network of loved ones and other supportive individuals can be vital to maintaining sobriety from porn addiction. These individuals can provide an individual with encouragement, guidance, and a sense of community as they work towards their recovery goals.

The Importance of Living a Fulfilling Life in Recovery

Living a fulfilling life in recovery from porn addiction is an essential aspect of long-term success in recovery. This may involve finding activities and pursuits that are meaningful and fulfilling and building healthy relationships and connections with others.

Several strategies can help you live a fulfilling life in recovery from porn addiction:

- ***Set goals:***

Goals can be vital to living a fulfilling life in recovering from porn addiction. These goals can be related to various aspects of an individual's life, such as personal growth, career, relationships, or health.

Setting and working towards goals can give an individual a sense of purpose and direction in their recovery journey.

- ***Find activities that are fulfilling and meaningful:***

Finding activities that are fulfilling and significant can be an essential aspect of living a fulfilling life in recovery from porn addiction. This may involve pursuing hobbies, volunteering, or engaging in other activities that bring joy and purpose to the person.

- ***Build healthy relationships:***

Building healthy relationships with others can be essential to living a fulfilling life in recovery from porn addiction. This may involve rebuilding damaged relationships or cultivating new connections with supportive individuals. Individuals must prioritize healthy communication, trust, and boundary-setting in their relationships.

- ***Practice gratitude:***

Practicing gratitude can be essential to living a fulfilling life in recovery from porn addiction. It involves focusing on the positive aspects of one's life and being thankful for what one has. This can help individuals feel more positive and hopeful as they navigate recovery challenges.

However, seeking support, practicing self-care, building healthy habits, finding purpose and always being grateful will help you maintain recovery and abstain from porn in the long term.

In summary, maintaining recovery from porn addiction can be a challenging process. Individuals may face temptations and triggers, as well as other challenges, as they work towards their goals.

Achieving Lasting Recovery and Creating a Fulfilling, Rewarding Life in Sobriety

Achieving lasting recovery and creating a fulfilling, rewarding life in sobriety requires a commitment to ongoing self-improvement and a willingness to make positive changes. Recovery is a lifelong process, and it's essential to understand that it's not just about stopping an addictive substance or behavior but about creating a new way of life.

A critical aspect of achieving lasting recovery is developing a solid support system. This can include participating in support groups, seeking out the support of friends and family, and working with a therapist or counselor.

A strong support system can provide encouragement, guidance, and accountability, which can be essential for maintaining sobriety.

It's also essential to develop healthy coping mechanisms. Addiction can be a coping mechanism for dealing with difficult emotions and situations, so finding healthy alternatives is necessary.

This can include engaging in activities you enjoy, practicing self-care, and developing healthy coping mechanisms such as mindfulness, journaling, and exercise.

Another critical aspect of lasting recovery is setting goals and working towards them. This goal-setting plan can include setting short-term and long-term goals and working towards them consistently and intentionally.

Setting goals can provide a sense of direction and purpose, which can be essential for maintaining motivation and drive towards change.

Achieving lasting recovery also includes addressing underlying emotional and psychological issues that may have contributed to the development of addiction, such as trauma and low self-esteem.

Some ways you can address underlying emotional and psychological problems include therapy, support groups, and self-help techniques.

By addressing these underlying issues, individuals can begin to heal and move towards lasting recovery.

It's important to remember that recovery is a lifelong process and requires ongoing effort and commitment. It's also important to be kind and compassionate with oneself, to celebrate small successes along the way, and to reflect on progress made.

Developing a solid support system, developing healthy coping mechanisms, setting goals and working towards them, addressing underlying emotional and psychological issues, and committing to ongoing self-improvement, can all aid in achieving lasting recovery and creating a fulfilling and rewarding life in sobriety.

In conclusion, achieving lasting recovery and creating a fulfilling, rewarding life in sobriety requires a commitment to ongoing self-improvement and a willingness to make positive changes.

Conclusion

Throughout the book, I explored various aspects of the journey to overcoming porn addiction, including the definition and symptoms of addiction, the causes and consequences of addiction, and strategies for overcoming addiction and rebuilding trust in relationships.

I have also emphasized the importance of seeking help for porn addiction. This help can be in the form of support from a therapist, support group, or loved ones and engaging in various treatment approaches, such as cognitive-behavioral or dialectical behavior therapy.

Maintaining recovery from porn addiction can be challenging, and an individual needs to be patient and persistent in their efforts. Strategies such as seeking support, practicing self-care, building healthy habits, finding meaning and purpose, and practicing gratitude can help you stay on track in recovery.

Living a fulfilling life in recovery from porn addiction is an essential aspect of long-term success in recovery. This may involve finding activities and pursuits that are meaningful and fulfilling and building healthy relationships and connections with others.

Despite the challenges encountered on the journey to overcoming porn addiction, it is possible to overcome addiction and achieve lasting recovery. With the right resources and support, individuals suffering from porn addiction can build a healthy and fulfilling life in recovery.

In conclusion, overcoming porn addiction is a challenging but ultimately rewarding process. With the right resources and support, individuals can overcome addiction and build a healthy and fulfilling life in recovery. I hope this book has provided you with helpful information and strategies for your journey towards health and healing.

Epilogue:

As you have journeyed through this book, "Freedom from Porn Addiction: A Journey to Health and Healing," you have learned about the causes and effects of porn addiction, as well as strategies for overcoming it. You have explored the importance of self-care, self-compassion, and addressing underlying emotional and psychological issues. You have also learned about relapse prevention and maintaining recovery.

Recovering from a porn addiction is not easy, and it's important to remember that it's a lifelong process. It requires effort, commitment, and patience. It's important to be kind and compassionate with oneself and to celebrate small successes along the way.

It's also important to remember that recovery is not just about stopping the use of porn, but about creating a new way of life. This can include setting goals, developing healthy coping mechanisms, building a strong support system, and addressing underlying emotional and psychological issues.

We hope that this book has provided valuable information and guidance for your journey towards freedom from porn addiction. Remember that recovery is possible and you are not alone. There are many resources available to support you on your journey, including therapy, support groups, and self-help techniques.

We wish you the best of luck on your journey towards health and healing. Remember to be patient and compassionate with yourself, and to keep moving forward.

About the Author

Susan J. McKinney is a Health Professional and Psychologist with over 7 years of experience in the field of addiction and recovery. She has helped countless individuals overcome addiction and improve their overall well-being. Susan is passionate about spreading awareness and providing support for those affected by addiction.

THE END